hot drinks

Indulgent hot chocolates, great coffees, soothing teas,
spiced punches, and other warming treats for cold days

hot drinks

with recipes by
LOUISE PICKFORD

with photography by William Lingwood

RYLAND
PETERS
& SMALL

LONDON NEW YORK

First published in the
United States in 2008 by
Ryland Peters & Small Inc.
519 Broadway
5th Floor
New York
NY 10012
USA

www.rylandpeters.com

10 9 8 7 6 5 4 3 2 1

Library of Congress Cataloging-in-Publication Data

Pickford, Louise.
  Hot drinks : indulgent hot chocolates, great
coffees, soothing teas, spiced punches, and other
warming treats for cold days / with recipes by
Louise Pickford and photography by William
Lingwood. -- 1st ed.
       p. cm.
  Includes index.
  ISBN 978-1-84597-804-4
  1. Beverages. I. Title.
  TX815.P53 2008
  641.2--dc22

                                    2008010330

Printed and bound in China

Designer Paul Tilby

Commissioning Editor Julia Charles

Production Toby Marshall

Art Director Leslie Harrington

Publishing Director Alison Starling

Indexer Hilary Bird

Notes

• All spoon measurements are level unless
otherwise stated.

• All eggs are medium, unless otherwise specified.
It is generally recommended that free-range eggs
be used. Recipes containing raw or partially
cooked egg should not be served to the very
young, very old, anyone with a compromised
immune system, or pregnant women.

Contents

For most of us around the world a hot drink is a daily ritual. Whether this is morning coffee, afternoon tea, or a soothing nightcap, it has become ingrained in our lives more so perhaps than any other food or beverage on the planet. While both tea and coffee in all their various forms are the most widely consumed hot drinks, there is a huge variety of other beverages we like to prepare and serve warm or hot, either alcoholic versions, such as mulled wines, or milk-based drinks infused with herbs, spices, and aromatics.

Some like it hot...

This book is a collection of flavored coffees, teas, hot chocolates, alcoholic drinks, and milk concoctions guaranteed to stimulate mind, body, or soul—often all three at once. As many are stimulants their appeal is instantly recognizable. But it is not just the satisfaction we gain physically from these drinks that makes them so attractive, there is often an emotional and nostalgic attachment stemming from childhood or festive occasions when many drinks come into their own.

We often associate hot drinks with colder climates, yet culturally and historically this isn't necessarily so. For sure, many of the mulled spiced wines such as Glühwein (or glow wine) originate from Germany and other eastern European and Scandinavian countries where getting warm quickly is essential during the bitterly cold winter months. However, the majority of hot drinks hail from warm climes. Coffee was first discovered in Ethiopia and quickly traveled to the Middle East, chocolate (or cocoa) was cultivated as far back as 1000 BC by the Mayans and Aztecs in Mexico, and the tea ceremonies of China and Japan are likewise steeped in a fascinating history, with cultivation of tea dating back to 1100 BC.

The benefits of consuming hot drinks are many, yet for me their greatest appeal, especially of those I drink less regularly, say at Christmas or other holiday occasions, is most definitely one of satisfaction. This pleasure is derived not only from the drinking but often from the process of gently warming and stirring various combinations until they almost reach a boil. With so many wonderful hot drinks to choose from in this book, you should find something delicious to drink on any occasion throughout the year.

The book is divided into chapters determined by the main ingredient of each recipe. The first chapter, **Coffees**, includes several timeless classics from around the world, including Irish Coffee and Turkish Coffee as well as some more unusual and innovative drinks such as Pumpkin Latte and Mocha Maple Coffee. Tips on coffee making can be found in individual recipes.

Teas and Infusions combine traditional teas such as Japanese Green Tea and the evocative Spiced Chai Masala from India. Some wonderfully restorative and calming infusions too, like Mint or Rosemary Tisane and the wonderfully perfumed Lavender Tea are also included.

For all chocoholics out there, **Hot Chocolates** contains a fabulous selection of rich and comforting hot chocolate drinks, once again inspired by beverages from around the globe. Classic recipes include The Finest Hot Chocolate by chocolate guru Linda Collister as well as some tempting new ideas such as Peppermint White Chocolate Dream and the exceedingly decadent Hot Chocolate Cups with Whipped Almond Cream.

As the days get shorter and the chill of winter starts to bite, what could be more inviting than the idea of sipping warmed **Punches and Cocktails** in front of a roaring fire? Although many of the mulled drinks tend to be associated with Christmas, thanks to their earthy spices and festive flavors, there are many others that have no such seasonal restrictions. Caribbean Café with Rum and Malibu adds an exotic twist to after-dinner coffee, while the healing properties of a Hot Toddy will help ward off a cold any time of the year.

The last chapter, **Milk Drinks**, is bound to be a hit with the entire family as it includes plenty of delicious milk drinks that kids will love. Ideal for bedtime is the appropriately named Sleep Tight Milk, with the soothing effects of lavender and restorative properties of honey, while the Peanut Butter Crunch is a wickedly sweet and indulgent treat for children and grown-ups alike.

You will need little specialized equipment to make any of the drinks in this book. Coffee machines come in many shapes and sizes and I recommend you use the one you are most familiar with. Other than that, Turkish Coffee (see page 10) is traditionally made using a cezve—a special copper pot with a lip on one side and a handle on the other, but the coffee can easily be made in a small saucepan. For the recipes that call for espresso, you can use a coffee machine or an inexpensive stovetop coffee maker that's widely available. Teapots too come in different shapes and sizes and if you are anything like me you'll have more than one. Other than that, you just need a saucepan and a method of heating liquid and you can make any of the drinks in this book.

coffees

Really good coffee

Proper coffee is very easy to make. You don't need special pots or hissing machines, just a heatproof pitcher and a fine tea strainer. Hot milk makes all the difference for those who take milk in their coffee; it produces a drink that is almost velvety and one that keeps hot. Freshly ground coffee is important (freeze the bag after opening, then use straight from frozen.) Espresso coffee will take a little longer to settle.

4 heaping tablespoons medium-ground coffee

2½ cups just-boiled water

hot milk, to taste

SERVES 2

Pour some hot water into a heatproof pitcher to warm it up. Empty out and add the coffee. Pour on enough recently boiled water just to cover the coffee grounds. Stir and leave for 1 minute to infuse. Top up with the just-boiled water and stir well. Cover and let brew for 5 minutes.

Either strain through a tea strainer into cups or into another warmed pitcher. Add hot (not boiled) milk, if using. The coffee will have a "crema" or creamy foam on top if you have followed all the steps correctly, and will have a full, rich flavor.

Turkish coffee

When brewing Turkish coffee there are several important points to remember. First you will need very finely ground coffee (or grind it yourself until it's finer than espresso coffee grounds), a small pot to heat the coffee and water together, traditionally called a "cezve." This is a small copper pot with a lip on one side and handle on the other (see picture right). Finally never take your eyes off the heating process; if the mixture boils over it makes quite a mess. In Turkey coffee is nearly always sweetened, but is optional.

Put the water in a small saucepan (preferably a Turkish coffee pot, see recipe introduction) and stir in the ground coffee and sugar, if using. Heat very gently until the coffee just reaches boiling point.

Pour enough coffee into 2 small coffee cups to come about halfway up, then reheat the remaining coffee until it almost boils again. Add the remaining coffee to the cups and let stand for 1 minute before drinking. Sweeten with sugar if you like.

2½ cups cold water

2 teaspoons extra-finely ground coffee

sugar, to taste (optional)

SERVES 2

Moroccan spiced coffee

1 cinnamon stick, crumbled

seeds from 3 green cardamom pods

¼ teaspoon fennel seeds

2 teaspoons toasted sesame seeds

2 oz. medium-ground coffee

2 cups just-boiled water

milk and sugar, to taste

This is a lovely aromatic coffee with spices and the unusual addition of ground toasted sesame seeds—these add a wonderful nutty flavor to the coffee. This recipe makes 2 large or 4 small cups.

Put the spices and sesame seeds in a spice grinder and grind finely. Stir into the ground coffee and use this mixture to make coffee in your preferred method adding milk and/or sugar if you like.

SERVES 2–4

Thai coffee

⅔ cup sweetened condensed milk, at room temperature

1½ cups freshly brewed strong, hot coffee

SERVES 2

Coffee in Thailand is often served iced but can be served hot too. It is always very sweet as it is served over sweetened condensed milk. You can either stir the coffee and milk together or drink the hot coffee first and then enjoy the warm milk underneath (see picture right).

Divide the condensed milk between 2 heatproof glasses then very carefully pour in the coffee so that it sits on top of the milk. Stir if you like, then drink straight away.

variation Add a little freshly ground cardamom and coriander to the ground coffee before brewing.

Spicy Arabic coffee

Coffee is a symbol of Arab hospitality, served black and in tiny cups, with as many refills as you can handle. Poured from elegant, long-spouted coffee pots with a cardamom pod wedged in the spout, the coffee comes out in a fragrant arc.

4 heaping tablespoons coarse-ground coffee

1½ teaspoons cardamom seeds, plus 4 whole green cardamom pods, bruised

4–5 cups just-boiled water

1 teaspoon rosewater or orange flower water

light brown sugar, to serve (optional)

SERVES 6

Put the ground coffee and cardamom in a large saucepan, then add 5 cups boiling water (if you prefer even stronger coffee, use only 4 cups). Add the rosewater or orange flower water and return to a boil. Reduce the heat and simmer for 1 minute, then turn off the heat. Cover with a lid and let infuse for about 30 minutes.

Before serving, gently warm the coffee without boiling, then transfer to a warmed coffee pot. Pour into small espresso cups and serve with sugar, if using.

Affogato

"Affogato" means "drowned" in Italian and here refers to a wonderful hot/cold drink often served as a dessert, where scoops of vanilla ice cream are drowned with a shot of hot espresso. This version takes the drink a step further with the addition of whipped cream and cocoa powder.

Put a scoop of ice cream in each of 2 heatproof glasses or cups and pour a shot of espresso into each one. Top with a little whipped cream and serve dusted with cocoa powder.

variation Replace the vanilla ice cream with chocolate ice cream for a delicious mocha affogato.

2 scoops vanilla ice cream

2 shots freshly brewed hot espresso coffee

⅓ cup whipping cream, whipped

cocoa powder, to dust

SERVES 2

Irish coffee

The trick to this popular digestif is not to go crazy with the heavy cream. Sweetening the coffee does help the cream sit well, but if you don't take sugar it should still work—you'll just need a steadier hand.

2½ oz. whiskey

4 shots freshly brewed hot espresso coffee

4 teaspoons simple syrup

½ cup heavy cream

6 coffee beans, to serve

SERVES 2

Mix the whiskey, coffee, and sugar, to taste, in heatproof glasses, making sure the coffee is piping hot. Slowly layer the cream over the surface of the coffee, using a flat-bottomed barspoon or a teaspoon. Decorate with three coffee beans and serve immediately.

Mocha maple coffee

Coffee and chocolate make perfect partners as this delicious drink proves. The addition of sweet, maple-flavored cream makes this an indulgent treat and the perfect after-dinner drink.

Pour the freshly brewed coffee into 2 heatproof glasses and add a shot of crème de cacao or chocolate syrup to each one.

Lightly whisk the cream and maple syrup together until the mixture is foaming and thickened slightly. Slowly layer the cream over the surface of the coffee using a flat-bottomed barspoon or a teaspoon. Sprinkle with grated chocolate and serve immediately.

2 cups freshly brewed hot coffee

2 shots crème de cacao or chocolate syrup

½ cup whipping cream

1 teaspoon maple syrup

grated bittersweet chocolate, to sprinkle

SERVES 2

Mochaccino

Strong espresso coffee is combined here with chocolate to make a delicious and rich-tasting mocha drink.

Grate the chocolate and put it in 2 small cups. Pour a shot of hot espresso into each one. Stir well until the chocolate is melted. Meanwhile, heat the milk in a small saucepan until hot then use a milk frother or balloon whisk to froth the milk. Pour it over the coffee and top with whipped cream, coffee beans, and a sprinkle of grated chocolate. Serve immediately.

2 oz. bittersweet chocolate

2 shots freshly brewed hot espresso coffee

1 cup milk

½ cup whipping cream, whipped

chocolate-coated coffee beans and grated bittersweet chocolate, to serve

SERVES 2

Vanilla coffee

I find that grinding freshly roasted coffee beans with chopped vanilla beans produces a lovely, naturally flavored coffee with just the right aroma and taste. Once ground, use at once or keep in a screw-top jar until ready to use.

1 oz. coffee beans

2 vanilla beans, roughly chopped

milk and sugar, to taste (optional)

SERVES 4

Put the coffee beans and vanilla beans in a coffee grinder and grind finely. Use this mixture to make coffee in your preferred method adding milk and/or sugar if you like.

Pumpkin latte

Perfect for Halloween, this thick, richly spiced latte is flavored with sweetened pumpkin. You can use canned sweetened pumpkin purée, but if you do use it, omit the sugar in the recipe.

Put the milk, pumpkin, sugar (if using), and cinnamon in a saucepan and heat gently, whisking constantly until the mixture just reaches boiling point. Transfer to 3 cups or heatproof glasses and stir in the coffee. Serve topped with lightly whipped cream and a dusting of cinnamon sugar.

1½ cups milk

3½ oz. cooked sweet pumpkin, mashed or canned pumpkin purée

3 tablespoons brown sugar (omit if using canned purée)

¼ teaspoon ground cinnamon

1 cup freshly brewed hot coffee

whipped cream and cinnamon sugar, to serve

SERVES 3

Egg-nog latte

This warming, festive drink with a hint of coffee makes a lovely alternative to the more traditional egg nog. For a non-alcoholic version, omit the rum.

2 cups milk

1 vanilla bean, split

2 very fresh eggs

2–3 tablespoons superfine sugar, to taste

½ teaspoon ground cinnamon

a pinch of grated nutmeg

2 tablespoons dark rum

1 cup freshly brewed hot coffee

SERVES 4

Put the milk and vanilla bean in a saucepan and heat gently until the milk just reaches boiling point. Meanwhile, put the eggs, sugar and spices in a bowl and whisk until frothy. Stir in the milk, then return the mixture to the pan. Heat gently for 2–3 minutes, stirring constantly with a wooden spoon, until the mixture thickens slightly. Remove from the heat and stir in the rum and coffee. Pour into 4 heatproof glasses and serve immediately.

teas and infusions

Lavender tea

The very essence of a hot summer afternoon in Italy or the South of France, lavender tea is wonderfully calming for frazzled nerves. Drink it to relax after a hard day at the office, or sip a cup before going to bed to aid sleep.

1–2 large sprigs of lavender leaves

a few lavender flowers, if available

1–2 teaspoons honey, to taste (optional)

SERVES 1

Put the lavender leaves and flowers (if using) in a one-cup French press and fill with boiling water. Cover and let infuse for about 5 minutes. Put 1 teaspoon honey, if using, in a cup, then carefully press down the plunger and pour the tea over the top.

Alternatively, pour the honey (if using) over the lavender in the French press before adding the boiling water.

Rosemary tisane

"Tisane" is a French word which means an infusion of herbs, flowers, or leaves, usually dried. In early times, they were seen as cures for many ailments. Nowadays, people drink them because they taste good. A tisanière is a tall, lidded cup, with a strainer inside to hold the herb. If you don't have one, use a small French press instead.

Put the rosemary and honey in a one-cup French press and cover with boiling water. Cover and let infuse for about 5 minutes, then carefully press down the plunger and pour the tisane into cups.

variations Tisanes can also be made with camomile flowers, lemon balm, marjoram, sage, thyme, or orange blossoms.

4–6 sprigs of rosemary

1–2 teaspoons honey

SERVES 1–2

Indian chai masala

This spiced Indian tea has become popular in the West—not surprising as it's a delicious and reviving drink.

Mix the spices well. Put the water, milk, and sugar in a saucepan. Add the tea and spices. Bring to a boil, reduce the heat and simmer for 2 minutes. Strain into 2 cups and serve immediately.

variation Try altering the spice mixture to suit your own taste. Use ground ginger if making a larger quantity.

½ cup milk

1 cup water

2 teaspoons sugar

1 teaspoon black tea

¼ teaspoon freshly grated nutmeg

¼ teaspoon finely grated fresh ginger or a pinch of ground ginger

3 cloves

seeds from 3 green cardamom pods

a pinch of ground cinnamon

SERVES 2

Lime blossom tea

In June and July in the Drôme region of France people gather the fuzzy yellow blossom from lime trees. The tea made from it is said to promote sleep and good digestion, and to be a remedy for migraine. It also tastes delightful.

Put the lime blossoms in a saucepan, add the water and heat until nearly boiling. Turn off the heat and let infuse for 3–4 minutes.

Put 1 teaspoon honey into each of 4 tea glasses or cups and strain in the tea. Stir with licorice twigs (if using) and drink hot.

1 handful of fresh lime blossoms, crushed, or ½ handful of dried lime tea

2 cups water

4 teaspoons honey

4 stems dried licorice twigs (optional)

SERVES 4

North African mint tea

The North African way is to pour this tea from a great height, creating bubbles on the surface of the drink. It is traditionally drunk in small, often decorative, tea glasses that are frequently replenished, and accompanied by delicious, sticky-sweet pastries.

Rinse a teapot with boiling water to warm it. Add the green tea and mint. Pour in the water and let infuse for 3 minutes. Strain into 2 heatproof glasses or cups then stir in sugar, to taste. Put the pine nuts in the glasses, if using. They soften as they soak and can be eaten at the end.

4 teaspoons Chinese green tea, such as gunpowder

2 sprigs of fresh mint, ideally spearmint

2 cups just-boiled water

½–2 teaspoons superfine sugar, to taste

a small handful of pine nuts (optional)

SERVES 2

Lemon verbena tea

1 handful of dried lemon verbena leaves or ½ handful fresh ones, crushed

4 slices of lemon or lime

4 white sugar lumps

SERVES 4

Herbalists, naturopaths, gourmands, and French gardeners have used the leaves of the lemon-scented verbena shrub for centuries: the aroma and taste are sharp but refreshing. Drink this infusion in the morning as a restorative after rich or spicy food the night before. Cooled and served over ice, this recipe also makes a refreshing summer drink.

Rinse a teapot with boiling water to warm it. Add the leaves and top up with near-boiling water. Let infuse for 3–5 minutes. Put a lemon slice and a sugar lump into each of 4 tea glasses or cups. Pour in the tea and drink hot.

Cardamom green tea

In India, tea is usually made with milk (see Indian Chai Masala page 26), but in the far north, which had trading links with China, they sometimes use green tea. This recipe contains an aromatic treasure—a spoonful of green cardamom pods. Often you find a few pods stuffed down the spout of the teapot, so the boiling tea picks up gorgeous flavors as it passes over the spice. Like ginger, cardamom is also a soothing agent for upset stomachs.

Rinse a teapot with boiling water to warm it. Add the tea and cardamom, then pour in the boiling water. Let infuse for 1–2 minutes (no longer, or the tea will taste bitter). Pour the tea and add sugar only if you usually like sweet tea.

3 teaspoons green tea

6–10 green cardamom pods

2 cups just-boiled water

sugar, to taste (optional)

SERVES 2

Star anise tea

2 good-quality tea bags

2 star anise

sugar, to taste

milk (optional)

SERVES 2

If you like aniseed flavors, like licorice or pastis, you'll love this drink. Tea is always best made with leaves, but this recipe can also be made with your favorite brand of tea bag. I like it not too strong and served without milk.

Put 1 tea bag and 1 star anise into each of 2 cups, add sugar if you usually use it, then pour over just-boiled water to fill. Let brew for your usual amount of time, then remove the tea bag and serve with milk (if using).

Hot lemon tea

1 lemon

2 tablespoons honey

1 pot freshly brewed black tea of your choice

SERVES 2

If you order a cup of tea in Italy you will get a hot lemon tea—adding milk is considered rather eccentric! Why not try this for a refreshing change.

Cut 2 slices off the lemon and squeeze the juice from the rest. Divide the honey between 2 large cups, add a lemon slice and half the lemon juice to each, then top up with hot tea. Stir as the honey melts and serve.

Spiced winter tea

A deliciously fragrant tea that's especially reviving after a long winter's walk, you can make this as strong or as weak as you like. Try adding a teaspoon of condensed milk to each cup—if you do so, there's no need for extra sugar.

Put the cinnamon, cloves, star anise, and cardamom pods in a saucepan, add the water and bring to a boil. Reduce the heat, cover and simmer gently for 5 minutes, then add the loose tea. Stir well, cover and let infuse for 5 minutes. Strain into a warmed teapot, and serve with sugar or condensed milk (if using).

1 cinnamon stick

3 cloves

1 star anise

3–4 green cardamom pods, lightly crushed

4 cups water

1 heaping tablespoon Indian leaf tea, such as Darjeeling or Assam

sugar, to taste (optional)

4–6 teaspoons sweetened condensed milk (optional)

SERVES 4-6

Ginger and lemon tisane

This lightly spiced tisane has a wonderful cleansing effect on the body and makes an ideal start to the day.

1-inch piece of fresh ginger, peeled

1 lemongrass stalk

2 teaspoons honey

4 lemon slices

SERVES 2

Thinly slice the ginger and cut the lemongrass stalk in half crosswise, then lengthwise. Divide the ginger and lemongrass between 2 cups, then add the honey and the slices of lemon. Top up with boiling water and serve.

Fresh mint tisane

This refreshing tisane is ideal after a rich meal as it calms and aids digestion.

1 large bunch of fresh mint

sugar or honey, to taste (optional)

SERVES 2-4

Wash the mint well and reserve a few leaves for serving. Put the remainder in a large French press. Top up with boiling water, let infuse for 3–5 minutes, then carefully press down the plunger. Pour into tea glasses, add sugar or honey (if using) and the reserved mint leaves, then serve.

Fresh ginger tea

Fresh ginger is an old folk remedy for colds, so this spicy tea is ideal for the winter months. Like cardamom, ginger is also very good for upset stomachs so it can be particularly helpful in treating morning sickness or seasickness.

1-inch piece of fresh ginger, peeled and grated

2 teaspoons black leaf tea

sugar or honey, to taste

SERVES 1

Put the grated ginger in a tea strainer or tea ball set in a cup, then add the tea. Pour in enough boiling water to cover the tea, then, let infuse for 1–5 minutes, according to how strong you like the flavor. Sweeten to taste with sugar or honey and sip slowly.

note If you're short of time, you don't need to grate the ginger—just slice it into a cup, then add boiling water.

hot chocolates

Hot chocolate with chile

Use the best quality cocoa powder you can find, preferably Dutch process.
The heat of the chile takes this chocolate drink to another dimension!

2 teaspoons cocoa powder

**2½ cups whole milk, or
1¼ cups milk mixed with
1¼ cups light cream**

**1 teaspoon chopped dried
chile or ½ teaspoon
chopped fresh red chile**

sugar, to taste (optional)

SERVES 2

Put the cocoa powder in a heatproof bowl, add about
1 tablespoon of the milk and mix to a smooth paste with
a wooden spoon.

Put the remaining milk or milk and cream mixture in a saucepan,
add the chile, and bring to a boil. Carefully strain the boiling milk
onto the cocoa paste through a fine-mesh strainer, then whisk
vigorously. Pour into 2 cups. Let cool for about 1 minute, then
taste—you may need to add sugar. Serve immediately.

The finest hot chocolate

The ultimate hot chocolate drink—the best quality chocolate, a hint of vanilla, lots of frothy milk topped with whipped cream, and grated chocolate. This is what chocolate lovers have been waiting for. Make sure the cups are warmed beforehand.

Put the chocolate pieces, sugar, vanilla bean, and milk in a saucepan. Heat gently, stirring, until the chocolate has melted, then bring to a boil, whisking constantly with a balloon whisk, until very smooth and frothy. Remove the vanilla bean.

Pour into 2 warmed cups, top with whipped cream and a sprinkling of grated chocolate or cocoa and serve immediately.

3 oz. bittersweet chocolate, broken into pieces

1 tablespoon superfine sugar, or to taste

1 vanilla bean, split lengthwise

1¼ cups milk

⅓ cup heavy cream or whipping cream, whipped

grated chocolate or cocoa powder, to sprinkle

SERVES 2

Pistachio-topped chocolate

The addition of pistachio nuts to this rich, creamy hot chocolate adds a lovely flavor and texture. Toasted hazelnuts make a good alternative.

Put the chocolate in a heatproof bowl. Put the milk and cream in a saucepan and bring to a boil. Remove the pan from the heat and let the milk subside. Pour a small amount of the hot milk and cream over the chocolate and stir to form a smooth paste. Gradually pour in the remaining milk, stirring gently, until the chocolate has melted. Let infuse for several minutes.

Return the chocolate milk to the pan and reheat gently. Do not let it boil or it may separate. Remove the pan from the heat, whisk to a foam with a balloon whisk, then pour into 2 cups. Sprinkle the pistachios over the top of the foam and serve immediately.

2 oz. bittersweet chocolate, grated or finely chopped

1 cup milk

1 tablespoon heavy cream

½ teaspoon finely ground pistachio nuts

SERVES 2

Minted hot chocolate

Chocolate with a hint of after-dinner mints—just
the thing to send you off into a peaceful sleep,
or warm you up on a chilly winter's afternoon.

Put the milk and mint sprigs in a saucepan and heat very
gently until boiling. Boil for 1 minute, then remove from the
heat. Discard the mint.

Divide the chocolate between 2 cups. Pour in the hot milk and
stir until the chocolate has melted. Serve the sugar separately,
if using.

2 cups milk

**4 sprigs of fresh mint,
bruised lightly to extract
flavor**

**2 oz. bittersweet chocolate,
chopped**

sugar, to taste (optional)

SERVES 2

Monsieur St Disdiers' chocolate

1¼ cups water

**2 oz. bittersweet chocolate,
finely chopped**

**⅓ cup superfine sugar, or
to taste**

**2 large pinches of ground
cinnamon**

**½ vanilla bean, split
lengthwise**

SERVES 4

This French recipe was first recorded in 1692
and soon became a court favorite in England.
King William III enjoyed chocolate so much he
installed a special chocolate kitchen in the royal
apartments and Monsieur St Disdiers was the first
Royal Chocolate Maker. The froth was considered
very important—some cooks would add egg white
to increase the volume of the froth. It is incredibly
rich, so serve it in small quantities.

Put the water in a heavy-based saucepan, bring to a boil,
then remove from the heat and add the chocolate, sugar, and
cinnamon. Using the tip of a small knife, scrape the seeds from
the vanilla bean into the saucepan.

Using a balloon whisk, whisk constantly for a few minutes,
taking care not to splash the boiling liquid. When a good amount
of froth has been created, pour the chocolate into warmed cups,
then spoon the froth on top and serve.

John Nott's wine chocolate

This unusual drink was created in 1726 by the pastry cook John Nott at Syon House in England (the country house of the Dukes of Northumberland). It is extremely rich, so serve in small quantities. An aperitif glass is ideal as it allows the chocolate to be sipped slowly.

Put all the ingredients in a heavy-based saucepan and whisk well with a balloon whisk. Bring just to a boil, whisking constantly. Let cool slightly before pouring into 4 small aperitif glasses to serve.

1¾ cups ruby port

2 oz. bittersweet chocolate, finely grated

⅓ cup superfine sugar, or to taste

1 teaspoon cornstarch

SERVES 4

Cinnamon mocha

Dip long cinnamon sticks into melted chocolate, leave to set, then use to stir this special drink.

Put the chocolate, milk, sugar, and cinnamon in a heavy-based saucepan and heat gently, stirring constantly, until melted and smooth. Bring the mixture to a boil, whisking constantly with a balloon whisk, then remove from the heat and whisk in the coffee and brandy, if using.

Remove the cinnamon stick. Put the curls of orange peel in tall, warmed, heatproof glasses, pour over the hot mixture, add a chocolate-dipped cinnamon stick and serve immediately.

2 oz. bittersweet chocolate, broken into pieces

1 cup milk

1 tablespoon sugar

1 cinnamon stick

1¼ cups freshly brewed hot, strong coffee

2 tablespoons brandy (optional)

2 curls of orange peel

cinnamon sticks dipped in melted chocolate, to serve

SERVES 2

---

4 oz. bittersweet chocolate, broken into pieces

1 tablespoon superfine sugar, or to taste

1¼ cups milk

2 cups freshly brewed hot, strong coffee

½ cup heavy or whipping cream, whipped

SERVES 4

Classic mocha

This is a truly classic coffee-chocolate combination. For best results, use freshly brewed coffee.

Put the chocolate, sugar, and milk in a heavy-based saucepan and heat gently, stirring constantly, until melted and smooth. Bring to a boil, whisking constantly with a balloon whisk, then remove from the heat and whisk in the coffee. Pour into warmed cups, top with whipped cream and serve immediately.

variation To make an Iced Mocha follow the recipe above but omit the cream. Make up the mixture of chocolate, sugar, milk, and coffee as given, then let cool and chill. Fill tall, chilled glasses with ice cubes, then pour over the mocha drink and serve immediately.

Traditional Mexican chocolate with vanilla cream

Mexico is where the world's love affair with chocolate began. The Aztecs used the cacao bean only for the drink, making it with water, sometimes adding vanilla and even chiles. The Spanish conquistadors altered the recipe to include sugar, cinnamon, and supposedly anise and pepper, the latter presumably to replace the hotter chile. Today, Mexicans use real chocolate pieces made with sugar, cinnamon, and almonds.

To make the vanilla cream, put the cream in a bowl and whisk until light and fluffy with soft peaks. Slit the vanilla bean lengthwise and carefully scrape out all the seeds. Gently fold them into the cream.

To make the hot chocolate, put the chocolate in a heatproof bowl set over a saucepan of gently simmering water and melt (don't let the bowl touch the water or the chocolate will be spoiled). Pour the milk into a large saucepan and stir in the sugar and cinnamon. Heat until gently simmering—do not boil. Whisk a ladle of the milk into the melted chocolate, then pour the mixture back into the saucepan, whisking until smooth.

Ladle into 6 cups. Top each with a spoonful of vanilla cream and serve hot with a cinnamon stick stirrer, if using.

1 cup heavy cream

1 vanilla bean

4 oz. bittersweet chocolate, broken into pieces

6 cups milk

4 tablespoons sugar

2 teaspoons ground cinnamon

cinnamon sticks, to serve (optional)

SERVES 6

Spanish chocolate with churros

Churros are long, golden, fingerlike Spanish doughnuts, deep-fried and rolled in sugar whilst still hot. They are eaten for breakfast, dipped into fantastically thick hot chocolate.

To make the churros, sift the flour onto a sheet of waxed paper. Put the milk and water in a medium saucepan and bring to a boil. Pour in the flour and beat vigorously with a wooden spoon, stirring until the mixture just begins to pull away from the sides of the pan. Remove the pan from the heat and let cool a little. Add the eggs and beat until the paste is completely smooth and not too runny (you may not need all of the egg).

Spoon the mixture into a piping bag. Heat the oil in a deep-fat fryer or wok until a piece of dough sizzles as soon as it hits the oil. Pipe fingers of the mixture into the hot oil, snipping off 4-inch lengths with kitchen scissors. Fry the churros in batches of 4–6 until golden brown, then remove with a slotted spoon and drain on paper towels. Put some sugar on a plate and roll the churros in it to coat. Eat immediately, dipping them into the hot chocolate. Any leftover churros can be frozen and reheated in the oven.

To make the Spanish hot chocolate, put the milk and allspice in a small saucepan and bring to a boil. Add the chocolate and stir until melted, then whisk in the egg yolks. Stir over gentle heat until slightly thickened. Whisk with a hand-held blender or a cappuccino frother, until frothy. Pour into cups and serve hot.

churros (makes about 12)

3 cups all-purpose flour

1¼ cups milk

1¼ cups water

2 eggs, beaten

vegetable oil, for
deep-frying

superfine sugar or
confectioners' sugar,
to dust

spanish hot chocolate

1⅔ cups milk

¼ teaspoon allspice

4 oz. bittersweet chocolate,
grated

2 very fresh egg yolks

*a piping bag fitted with
a large, fluted tip*

a deep-fat fryer (optional)

SERVES 2

2 cups milk

4 star anise

a pinch of freshly grated nutmeg, plus extra to dust

3½ oz. white chocolate, finely grated

SERVES 2

Spiced white chocolate

The hint of Asian spice is lovely here with the white chocolate and makes a satisfying and warming drink that's just perfect for bedtime.

Put the milk, star anise, and nutmeg in a saucepan and bring slowly to a boil. Simmer gently for 5 minutes then remove from the heat and stir in the chocolate until melted. Let cool for 5 minutes then pour into 2 cups, dust with a little grated nutmeg and serve.

variation You could also use bittersweet chocolate in this drink.

Spiced rum chocolate

This is an instant mood lifter—make this drink when you are feeling a bit dejected and it cannot fail to lift your spirits. Watch out though—it is quite potent! If you are feeling utterly miserable, the only answer is to top it with whipped cream and sink into comfort oblivion.

Put the milk, chocolate, star anise, orange peel, and honey in a saucepan and heat gently, stirring constantly, until the chocolate has melted.

Remove the star anise and discard. Add the rum and Grand Marnier and liquidize in a blender or with a hand-held blender until completely smooth and frothy. Pour into warmed heatproof glasses. Add a cinnamon stick, if using, and top with whipped cream if desired. Serve immediately.

2½ cups milk

2½ oz. bittersweet chocolate, chopped

2 star anise

finely grated peel of ½ an orange

1 tablespoon orange-blossom or acacia honey

2½ oz. spiced dark rum

1½ oz. Grand Marnier, Cointreau, or other orange-flavored liqueur

cinnamon sticks and whipped cream, to serve (optional)

SERVES 2

Hot chocolate cups with whipped almond cream

This is a rich, decadent chocolate drink topped with whipped, almond-flavored cream. Almond syrup is widely available in stores, alternatively you could use a few drops of almond extract.

Put the milk and cream in a saucepan and heat until almost boiling. Add the chocolate and stir over a low heat until the chocolate is completely melted. Remove from the heat and let sit for 5 minutes.

To make the almond cream, whip the cream and almond syrup together until thickened. Pour the chocolate milk into 4 small cups, spoon the almond cream on top and serve sprinkled with grated chocolate and slivered almonds.

1 cup milk

1 cup light cream

3½ oz. bittersweet chocolate, grated

grated chocolate and slivered almonds, to serve

whipped almond cream

½ cup heavy cream

1 teaspoon almond syrup

SERVES 4

Peppermint white chocolate dream

2 cups milk

3½ oz. white chocolate, chopped

½ teaspoon peppermint extract

½ cup heavy cream

grated white chocolate, to serve

SERVES 2

A soothing after-dinner drink is a perfect way to end your day. You can just as easily use bittersweet chocolate here if you prefer.

Put the milk, chocolate, and peppermint extract in a saucepan and heat gently until the chocolate is melted. Use a milk frother or balloon whisk to beat the mixture until it is light and foamy.

Divide between 2 heatproof glasses, whip the cream until thick, and spoon on top of the drinks. Sprinkle with a little grated white chocolate and serve immediately.

punches and cocktails

Hot toddy

5 cloves

2 lemon slices

2 oz. whiskey

1 oz. freshly squeezed lemon juice

2 teaspoons honey or sugar syrup, to taste

3 oz. just-boiled water

1 cinnamon stick, to serve (optional)

SERVES 1

The Hot Toddy, with its warming blend of spices and sweet honey aroma, is the perfect comforter and will soothe any aches, pains, or snuffles. It's also a great life-saver for cold afternoons spent outside watching sport. Next time you have need to pack a thermos of coffee, think again and mix up a batch of Hot Toddies—see how popular you are!

Skewer the cloves into the lemon slices and put them in a heatproof glass. Add the whiskey, lemon juice, and honey or sugar syrup to taste. Top up with boiling water and add a cinnamon stick to serve, if using.

Hot tea toddy

A variation of the classic Hot Toddy (see page 57), this comforting drink is especially good if you think you are coming down with a cold. Use decaffeinated tea for a bedtime drink.

Put the tea, cognac, rum, lemon zest, cloves, and honey in a saucepan and gently heat for 5 minutes without boiling. Remove from the heat, let infuse for 5 minutes. Strain into 2 cups or heatproof glasses and serve with a slice of lemon in each.

2 cups freshly brewed hot tea

4 tablespoons cognac

4 tablespoons dark rum

4 thinly pared strips of lemon peel

12 cloves

2–3 teaspoons honey, to taste

2 slices lemon, to serve

SERVES 2

Swedish glögg

"Glögg" is the Scandinavian version of Christmas "glühwein" or mulled wine. It's ideal for a party but you will need to get it started the day beforehand.

Using a vegetable peeler, remove the peel from the orange in a single curl (do not include any of the bitter white pith). Put all the ingredients except the almonds in a large stainless-steel or enamel saucepan and set aside overnight (at least 12 hours).

Just before serving, heat to just below boiling point. (Do not let the liquid reach a boil or the alcohol will be burned off.) Remove from the heat and stir in the almonds.

Serve in glass punch cups or tea glasses, with small spoons so that the softened almonds and raisins can be scooped out and eaten. Cinnamon sticks make attractive and scented stirrers.

1 orange

2 bottles dry red wine, 750 ml each

1 bottle aquavit or vodka, 750 ml

12 green cardamom pods, crushed

8 cloves

1-inch piece of fresh ginger, sliced

1 cinnamon stick

1½ cups sugar

1¼ cups raisins

1½ cups blanched almonds

cinnamon sticks, to serve (optional)

SERVES 20

Orange-mulled wine

If you've never made mulled wine yourself, you should try. It couldn't be simpler and tastes infinitely better than the ready-mixed versions. The only thing you have to be careful about is that the wine doesn't reach a boil.

Pour the wine and water into a large saucepan. Stud the orange with the cloves and add it to the pan, along with the lemon peel, spices, and sugar. Heat gently until almost boiling. Turn down to the lowest possible heat so that the liquid barely trembles and simmer for 30 minutes to let the spices infuse. Add the orange-flavored liqueur, then reheat gently.

Strain into a large, warmed bowl and float a few thin slices of orange on top. Ladle into small heatproof glasses or cups to serve.

2 bottles fruity red wine, 750 ml each

2 cups water

1 orange, plus a few extra slices to serve

a small handful of cloves

thinly pared peel of ½ a lemon

2 cinnamon sticks

6 green cardamom pods, lightly crushed

a little freshly grated nutmeg or a small pinch of ground nutmeg

½ cup soft brown sugar

3½ oz. Grand Marnier, Cointreau or other orange-flavored liqueur

SERVES 14–16

Blue blazer

A spectacular drink to serve but one that is best practised in the safe confines of the kitchen before trying it in front of an audience. There are a number of cocktails that can be created using a naked flame but these drinks are best kept for the start of the evening, for obvious reasons.

1 white sugar cube

2 oz. just-boiled water

2.oz whiskey

freshly grated nutmeg, to serve

Warm 2 small metal tankards. In one, dissolve the sugar in the boiling water. Pour the whiskey into the other. Set the whiskey alight using an extra-long match or a taper to keep your hands well away from the flame. As it burns, pour the liquid into the first tankard and back, from one to another, creating a continuous stream of fire. Once the flame has died down, pour the mixture into a warmed old-fashioned glass and sprinkle with nutmeg to serve.

SERVES 1

Mulled wine

2 bottles fruity red wine, 750 ml each

2 oranges

8 cloves

3 tablespoons brown sugar

2-inch piece of fresh ginger, peeled and chopped

1 cinnamon stick

½ teaspoon freshly grated nutmeg

SERVES 4-6

Warm your house and make your friends' hearts glow with this beautiful spicy drink. If you're making it for a big party, simply add more wine and sugar to the pan as the evening wears on.

Pour the red wine into a large saucepan. Stud the oranges with the cloves, then cut each orange into quarters. Add to the pan, together with the sugar, ginger, cinnamon, and nutmeg.

Heat the mixture to simmering point and simmer for 8–10 minutes. Ladle into small heatproof glasses or cups to serve.

Mulled cider

This makes such a delicious alternative to mulled wine that I'm not sure that I don't like it even better!

Put the hard cider, Calvados, and soft cider in a large saucepan. Add the sugar, lemon peel, cinnamon sticks, and cloves and heat very gently until the sugar has dissolved. Heat until almost at a boil, then turn off the heat, add the halved, dried apple slices and leave the mixture for 30 minutes to infuse.

Reheat, taking care not to let it reach a boil. Ladle into small heatproof glasses or cups to serve and add a piece of the dried apple to each.

2 cups hard apple cider

½ cup Calvados (French apple brandy) or brandy

3 cups soft apple cider or apple juice

⅓ cup soft brown sugar

a thinly pared strip of lemon peel

2 cinnamon sticks

8 cloves

6 slices of dried apple, halved

SERVES 10-12

Mulled bloody mary

This is totally delicious and tastes exactly as you'd imagine a warmed version of the classic brunch drink. It is perfect for a cold winter's morning, especially if you've over-indulged the night before!

Put the tomato juice in a saucepan. Cut half the lemon into slices and squeeze the juice from the remaining half into the pan. Add the lemon slices, Worcestershire sauce, and some salt and pepper to taste. Bring slowly to a boil and simmer gently, uncovered, for 10 minutes.

Remove the saucepan from the heat and let cool for about 20 minutes. Stir in the vodka and some celery salt to taste. Serve in tall heatproof glasses.

4 cups tomato juice

1 lemon

1–2 tablespoons Worcestershire sauce, to taste

3–4 oz. vodka

a pinch of celery salt

sea salt and freshly ground black pepper

SERVES 4-6

Egg nog

3 very fresh eggs

½ cup superfine sugar

3½ oz. bourbon

3½ oz. spiced rum

2⅓ cups milk

1 cup plus 2 tablespoons whipping cream

freshly grated nutmeg, to serve

SERVES 6-8

Once you've tasted this delicious light, foamy punch, I suspect you'll want to make it every year. This version is adapted from a recipe in top American bartender Dale Degroff's fabulous book "The Craft of the Cocktail."

Separate the egg yolks carefully from the whites and put them in separate large bowls. Beat the egg yolks with an electric hand-held whisk, gradually adding ¼ cup of the sugar, until they turn light in color and moussey in texture. Beat in the bourbon and spiced rum, then stir in the milk and cream.

Clean and dry the whisk thoroughly, then whisk the egg whites until beginning to stiffen. Add the remaining sugar and whisk again until they form soft peaks. Fold the whites into the egg nog mixture and grate over a little nutmeg. The egg nog can be served cold or gently heated in a large saucepan until just warm, as preferred. Ladle into small glasses or cups to serve.

Hot rum and cider punch

I love this fall drink with its slices of apple infused with the flavors of the hard cider, rum, and spices. It would make a great drink for a Halloween party. If you want to serve a family-friendly, non-alcoholic version, simply replace the hard cider with soft cider or apple juice and omit the rum.

Put the hard cider, lemon slices, apple slices, cinnamon, cloves, sugar, and rum in a saucepan and heat the mixture gently until it just reaches boiling point. Simmer very gently for 10 minutes, then remove from the heat and let infuse for 10 minutes. Ladle into small heatproof glasses or cups to serve.

2 cups hard apple cider

2 slices lemon

1 apple, cored and thinly sliced

1 cinnamon stick, crushed

3 cloves

2 tablespoons soft light brown sugar

3 oz. dark rum

SERVES 4–6

Portuguese mulled port

Similar to mulled wine but made using port, this is an elegant spiced punch perfect for a winter cocktail party. It is fairly potent so I like to serve it in small demitasse cups (or glasses) as an aperitif.

Peel and slice 1 orange and squeeze the juice from the second orange. Put the slices and juice in a saucepan and add the water, sugar, cloves, allspice, cinnamon stick, and nutmeg. Bring slowly to a boil, stirring until the sugar is dissolved.

Simmer gently for 10 minutes. Stir in the port and heat gently, without boiling, for a further 2–3 minutes. Strain and pour into small cups or heatproof glasses to serve.

2 oranges

2 cups water

¼ cup soft brown sugar

10 cloves, lightly crushed

6 allspice berries, crushed

1 cinnamon stick, crushed

¼ teaspoon freshly grated nutmeg

1 bottle ruby port, 750 ml

SERVES 12

Hot buttered rum

This is a simple mulled rum drink with the addition of butter to give it some extra richness. It's perfect for a chilly winter evening.

2 shots dark rum

4 cloves

2 lemon slices

2 teaspoons superfine sugar

1 cup just-boiled water

1 oz. butter

2 cinnamon sticks

SERVES 2

Put the rum into 2 heatproof glasses and add the cloves, lemon slices, and sugar. Top up with boiling water and add the butter. Put a cinnamon stick in each glass and use to stir the butter as it melts. Serve immediately.

Caribbean café
with rum and Malibu

2–4 teaspoons sugar, to taste

2 tablespoons dark rum

2 tablespoons Malibu

1 cup freshly brewed hot coffee

⅓ cup whipping cream

SERVES 2

This exotic flavored coffee is similar to an Irish coffee, where the alcohol and coffee are combined in a glass then lightly whipped cream is carefully poured on top over the back of a spoon so it floats on the surface. Traditionally you then drink the coffee through the layer of frothy cream.

Divide the sugar, rum, Malibu, and coffee between 2 heatproof glasses and stir well. Put the cream in a bowl and whisk until foaming. Slowly layer the cream over the surface of each coffee, using a flat-bottomed barspoon or a teaspoon. Serve immediately.

White Christmas

This is a delicious drink bursting with all the evocative flavors of the holiday season, such as orange and warming spices. For a large crowd, simply double or triple the ingredients as required. If you like frothy drinks (such as cappuccino), then a milk frother is an absolute must in your kitchen. There are various types available but basically they are devices that froth milk into foam until it is "stiff" enough to be spooned on top of a drink.

Put the milk, chocolate, orange, and spices in a saucepan and heat gently, stirring, until it just reaches boiling point. Froth the milk with a milk frother or whisk vigorously with a flat or small round whisk until the mixture is foamy.

Divide between 6 small cups or heatproof glasses and pour in the Grand Marnier. Spoon a little whipped cream on top of each drink and sprinkle with candied orange and grated white chocolate to serve.

4 cups milk

7 oz. white chocolate, grated

2 orange slices

4 cloves, lightly crushed

2 cinnamon sticks, lightly crushed

a pinch of freshly grated nutmeg

⅓ cup Grand Marnier or other orange-flavored liqueur

½ cup whipping cream, whipped

candied orange and grated white chocolate, to serve

SERVES 6

Polar bear

1 cup milk

1 cup heavy cream

3 oz. white chocolate, grated

⅓ cup Kahlúa or other coffee-flavored liqueur

½ cup whipping cream

grated white chocolate and white-chocolate-coated coffee beans, to serve

SERVES 2

Kahlúa is a coffee-flavored liqueur, which when combined with chocolate and cream looks innocent enough in a glass, but don't be deceived by looks—this deliciously creamy cocktail packs a punch! It's very rich and filling so it could easily be served as an alternative to dessert.

Put the milk and cream in a saucepan and heat gently until it just reaches boiling point. Remove the pan from the heat and stir in the chocolate until melted, then add the Kahlúa. Divide between 2 heatproof glasses or cups.

Whip the cream until thick, then spoon it over the drinks. Sprinkle with grated white chocolate and top with a few white-chocolate-coated coffee beans to serve.

Affogato liquore

2 scoops vanilla ice cream

2 shots freshly brewed
hot espresso coffee

2 shots Frangelico or other
Italian liqueur

SERVES 2

Here is a tempting alcoholic version of the Italian coffee with "drowned" ice cream. Frangelico is a delicious hazelnut liqueur from Northern Italy but you could use other Italian liqueurs, such as Amaretto di Saronno or Galliano.

Put the ice cream in 2 separate heatproof glasses or shallow dessert dishes. Pour a shot of coffee and a shot of liqueur over each one. Serve immediately with a spoon.

Catalan coffee punch

This is a traditional hot coffee and rum drink from the Catalonia region of Spain. The alcohol is burnt off before the coffee is added. It is traditional to use a terracotta cooking vessel for this, but a stainless-steel saucepan will work just as well. Be careful when igniting the rum. Use an extra-long match or a taper to keep your hands well away from the flame.

1 cup white rum

1–2 tablespoons
superfine sugar

1 cinnamon stick

2 thinly pared strips
of lemon peel

2 cups freshly brewed
hot coffee

SERVES 6-8

Put the rum, sugar, cinnamon, and lemon peel in a terracotta pot (or other flameproof dish) and carefully ignite the mixture. Let the flame die down completely then slowly pour in the hot coffee. Divide between heavy-based shot glasses or heatproof demitasse cups and serve.

milk drinks

Malted milk

There are several popular brands of malted milk available, but it is easy enough to make your own healthy version of this soothing bedtime drink.

Put the milk and malt extract in a saucepan and heat gently until it just reaches boiling point. Whisk the milk with a balloon whisk until frothy then pour it into 2 cups. Grate over a little nutmeg and serve.

2 cups milk

3 tablespoons barley malt extract

freshly grated nutmeg, to serve

SERVES 2

Vanilla soyaccino

For those who are lactose intolerant, soya milk is a good option. I love its nutty flavor and often drink it as an alternative to cow's milk. You can use dairy milk for this recipe if you prefer.

Put the milk, vanilla, and maple syrup in a saucepan and gently heat until it just reaches boiling point. Remove from the heat and then froth the milk, using a milk frother or balloon whisk. Pour it into 2 cups, dust with ground cinnamon or cocoa powder and serve immediately.

2 cups soya milk

1 teaspoon vanilla extract

4 teaspoons maple syrup

ground cinnamon or cocoa powder, to serve

SERVES 2

Babyccino

1 cup milk

2 teaspoons chocolate syrup or sauce

sweetened cocoa powder, to dust

mini marshmallows, to serve (optional)

SERVES 2

I always think it is cute when I see small children mimicking their parents with a "mini latte"—of course these are made without coffee but they look great with the drizzle of chocolate syrup inside the glass.

Put the milk in a saucepan and heat gently until warm, but not hot, then froth the milk using a milk frother or balloon whisk. Drizzle a little chocolate syrup inside 2 glasses and add the frothed milk. Dust with cocoa powder, top with the marshmallows, if using, and serve.

Marshmallow chocolate melt

2 cups milk

½ teaspoon vanilla extract

6 large marshmallows

1 oz. bittersweet chocolate, broken into pieces

SERVES 2

This is definitely a drink for those of you with a really sweet tooth!

Put the milk and vanilla extract in a saucepan and heat gently until it comes to a boil. Remove from the heat. Pour the milk into 2 cups and top with the marshmallows.

Meanwhile, melt the chocolate in a small heatproof bowl set over a pan of gently simmering water (don't let the bowl touch the water or the chocolate will be spoiled). Drizzle the melted chocolate over the top of the drinks and serve immediately.

Turkish delight frothy

You can use any flavor Turkish delight you like in this pretty, delicate drink. The best bit for me is finding half-melted pieces of the Turkish delight at the bottom of the cup! Serve with a spoon.

2 cups milk

2 oz. Turkish delight, cut into cubes, plus extra to top

½ cup whipping cream

2 teaspoons rosewater

½ teaspoon honey

a pinch of ground cardamom

unsalted pistachio nuts, finely chopped, to serve

SERVES 2

Put the milk and Turkish delight in a saucepan and heat gently, stirring constantly, until the mixture just reaches boiling point. Meanwhile, whip the cream, rosewater, honey, and ground cardamom in a bowl until just stiff. Pour the milk into 2 cups and top with the flavored cream. Sprinkle with pieces of Turkish delight and pistachio nuts and serve immediately.

Honey baba

2 cups milk

2 cinnamon sticks, lightly crushed

2 teaspoons honey

cinnamon sugar, to dust

SERVES 2

This is a delicately spiced milk drink infused with a hint of honey. You can always add a shot of rum to this for a grown-up version.

Put the milk and cinnamon sticks in a saucepan and heat gently until the mixture just reaches boiling point. Remove from the heat and strain well.

Add 1 teaspoon honey to each cup and pour in the cinnamon-infused milk. Dust with a little cinnamon sugar and serve immediately.

Sleep tight milk

Lavender soothes the body and mind which makes it the perfect ingredient for a bedtime drink. You can use either fresh or dried lavender flowers but remember if you use dried they are three times as strong, so use sparingly. If using fresh flowers or stems, make sure the lavender is free from pesticides (avoid those from nurseries). If you grow your own lavender, use that; dried lavender is available from specialty food stores.

2 cups milk

1 tablespoon lavender flowers (see recipe introduction)

2 teaspoons honey, preferably lavender

freshly grated nutmeg, to serve

SERVES 2

Put the milk, lavender, and honey in a saucepan and heat gently until the milk just reaches boiling point. Remove from the heat and let infuse for 10 minutes.

Strain the milk into 2 cups and serve dusted with a little freshly grated nutmeg.

Saffron milk

2 cups milk

¼ cup sweetened condensed milk

¼ teaspoon saffron threads, plus a few extra to serve

3 green cardamom pods, lightly crushed

SERVES 2

This drink is aromatic and exotic. The saffron, with its earthy flavor and striking color, is very pretty as well as delicious. The condensed milk does make this drink very sweet so, if you prefer, reduce the amount used and increase the quantity of milk.

Put the milk, condensed milk, saffron, and cardamom pods in a saucepan and heat gently, stirring constantly, until the mixture just reaches boiling point. Remove from the heat and let infuse for 5 minutes. Strain the milk into 2 heatproof glasses, sprinkle with a few saffron threads and serve immediately.

Rosemary milk

Rosemary may seem an unusual addition to a milk drink but not only is the flavor wonderful, rosemary has many health benefits too. It has long been known to soothe upset stomachs, aid digestion, and help prevent headaches. I love it simply for its interesting, aromatic flavor.

2 cups milk

2 large fresh rosemary sprigs, crushed

1–2 teaspoons soft brown sugar, to taste

SERVES 2

Put the milk and rosemary sprigs in a saucepan and heat very gently until it just reaches boiling point. Remove from the heat and let infuse for 5 minutes. Strain the milk into 2 cups, add sugar to taste and serve.

Warm banoffi smoothie

This is a delicious and fun way to enjoy a banana smoothie. You will need to drink it straight away as it becomes very thick if left for too long.

Put the bananas and milk in a blender or liquidizer and whizz until really smooth. Transfer the mixture to a saucepan and heat gently, stirring constantly, until it just reaches boiling point. Transfer to 2 cups or heatproof glasses, grate over a little nutmeg and add a swirl of toffee sauce.

2 bananas

2 cups milk

freshly grated nutmeg, to taste

toffee or caramel sauce, to serve

SERVES 2

Chocolate milk
with ice cream and chocolate drizzle

This is guaranteed to become a big favorite with the kids. You can top it with any flavor ice cream you like—chocolate or caramel work well.

2 tablespoons sweetened cocoa powder

500 ml milk

2 scoops vanilla ice cream

2 tablespoons chocolate syrup or sauce

SERVES 2

Mix the cocoa powder with about 2 tablespoons of the milk and mix to form a smooth paste. Gently heat the remaining milk in a saucepan until it just reaches boiling point and whisk into the chocolate mixture until evenly blended.

Divide between 2 cups and top each with a scoop of ice cream and some chocolate syrup. Serve immediately with spoons.

Spiced chile coconut milk

Coconut milk adds both a delicate flavor and wonderful creaminess to this spiced drink. The slight hint of chile is exotic and warming.

Put all the ingredients, except the heavy cream, in a saucepan. Heat gently for 10 minutes then bring just to boiling point. Strain into 2 cups.

Whip the cream until it holds its shape and spoon over the drinks. Sprinkle with a little toasted coconut to serve.

2 cups milk

2 cups coconut milk

1½ tablespoons soft brown sugar

2 star anise, lightly crushed

1 small red chile, halved lengthwise and seeded

½ cup heavy cream

toasted shredded coconut, to serve

SERVES 2

Peanut butter crunch

Another big hit with the kids, this is a deliciously creamy, nutty drink.

2 cups milk

3 tablespoons natural peanut butter

1 tablespoon maple syrup

¼ cup whipping cream

ground cinnamon, to serve

SERVES 2

Put the milk, peanut butter, and maple syrup in a saucepan and heat gently, stirring constantly, until it just reaches boiling point and the peanut butter has melted. Froth the mixture using a balloon whisk.

Divide between 2 heatproof glasses or cups. Whip the cream until it holds its shape and spoon over the drinks. Dust with a little cinnamon to serve.

Christmas milk

A slice of holiday fruit cake in a cup—yummy. The star decoration on top is fun, but optional, the drink tastes great either way!

Using the cookie cutter as a template, carefully draw a star on the card. Use scissors to cut out the star shape to create a stencil. Set aside until needed.

Put the milk raisins, ginger, honey, and orange slices in a saucepan. Heat gently until it just reaches boiling point. Divide the mixture between 4–6 cups. Lightly whip the cream until foaming and spoon it over the drinks.

Hold the stencil over each drink, making sure that the the star shape is in the center. Lightly dust with cinnamon sugar and remove the stencil to leave a star decoration on top. Repeat with all the drinks and serve immediately.

4 cups milk

4 tablespoons raisins

2 tablespoons chopped candied ginger

4 teaspoons clear honey

½ an orange, sliced

¼ cup whipping cream

cinnamon sugar, to dust

a piece of white card and a star-shaped cookie cutter, about 2-inches in diameter

SERVES 4–6

Index

conversion chart

Weights and measures have been rounded up
or down slightly to make measuring easier.

American	Metric	Imperial
6 tbsp butter	85 g	3 oz.
7 tbsp butter	100 g	3½ oz.
1 stick butter	115 g	4 oz.

Volume equivalents:

American	Metric	Imperial
1 teaspoon	5 ml	
1 tablespoon	15 ml	
¼ cup	60 ml	2 fl oz
⅓ cup	75 ml	2½ fl oz
½ cup	125 ml	4 fl oz
⅔ cup	150 ml	5 fl oz (¼ pint)
¾ cup	175 ml	6 fl oz
1 cup	250 ml	8 fl oz

Weight equivalents:

Imperial	Metric
1 oz	30 g
2 oz	55 g
3 oz	85 g
3½ oz	100 g
4 oz	115 g
6 oz	175 g
8 oz (½ lb)	225 g
9 oz	250 g
10 oz	280 g
12 oz	350 g
13 oz	375 g
14 oz	400 g
15 oz	425 g
16 oz (1 lb)	450 g

Measurements:

Inches	cm
¼ inch	0.5 cm
½ inch	1 cm
1 inch	2.5 cm
2 inches	5 cm
3 inches	7 cm
4 inches	10 cm
5 inches	12 cm
6 inches	15 cm
7 inches	18 cm
8 inches	20 cm
9 inches	23 cm
10 inches	25 cm
11 inches	28 cm
12 inches	30 cm

Oven temperatures:

120°C	(250°F)	Gas ½
140°C	(275°F)	Gas 1
150°C	(300°F)	Gas 2
170°C	(325°F)	Gas 3
180°C	(350°F)	Gas 4
190°C	(375°F)	Gas 5
200°C	(400°F)	Gas 6

Recipe credits

Louise Pickford

Affogato
Affogato liquore
Babyccino
Caribbean café with rum
and Malibu
Catalan coffee punch
Chocolate milk with ice cream
and chocolate drizzle
Christmas milk
Egg-nog latte
Ginger and lemon tisane
Honey baba
Hot buttered rum
Hot chocolate cups with whipped
almond cream
Hot rum and cider punch
Hot tea toddy
Malted milk
Marshmallow chocolate melt
Minted hot chocolate
Mocha maple coffee
Mochaccino
Moroccan spiced coffee
Mulled bloody Mary
Peanut butter crunch
Peppermint white
chocolate dream
Polar bear
Portuguese mulled port
Pumpkin latte
Rosemary milk
Saffron milk
Sleep tight milk

Spiced chile coconut milk
Spiced white chocolate
Thai coffee
Turkish coffee
Turkish delight frothy
Vanilla coffee
Vanilla soyaccino
Warm banoffi smoothie
White Christmas

Elsa Petersen-Schepelern

Cardamom green tea
Fresh ginger tea
Fresh mint tisane
Hot lemon tea
Lavender tea
Rosemary tisane
Star anise tea
Swedish glögg

Linda Collister

Cinnamon mocha
Classic mocha
The finest hot chocolate
John Nott's wine chocolate
Monsieur St Disdiers' chocolate

Maxine Clark

Really good coffee
Spanish hot chocolate
with churros
Spiced winter tea
Spiced rum chocolate

Fiona Beckett

Egg nog
Orange-mulled wine
Mulled cider

Ben Reed

Blue blazer
Hot toddy
Irish coffee

Hattie Ellis

Indian chai masala
North African mint tea

Clare Ferguson

Lemon verbena tea
Lime blossom tea

Manisha Gambhir Harkins

Spicy Arabic coffee
Traditional Mexican chocolate
with vanilla cream

Sara Jayne Stanes

Hot chocolate with chile
Pistachio-topped chocolate

Fran Warde

Mulled wine

Photography credits

All photographs by William Lingwood unless otherwise stated below:

Peter Cassidy
Pages 42, 48, 51, 60

Debi Treloar
Pages 27, 29, 63

Noel Murphy
Page 8

Martin Brigdale
Pages 41, 45, 46,

Richard Jung
Page 38

Ian Wallace
Page 35